PASSION: WHITE FLAG

PIANO / VOCAL / GUITAR

ISBN 978-1-4584-4066-2

7777 W. BLUEMOUND RD. P.O. BOX 13819 MILWAUKEE, WI 53213

Visit Hal Leonard Online at
www.halleonard.com

Not Ashamed

Words and Music by CHRIS TOMLIN,
MATT REDMAN, BRYAN BROWN
and TOFER BROWN

Capo 3 (C)

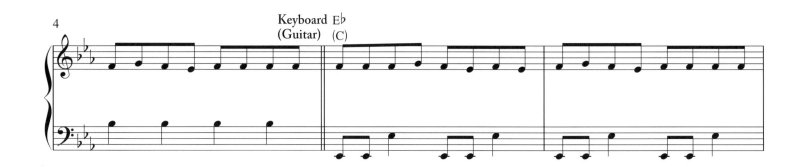

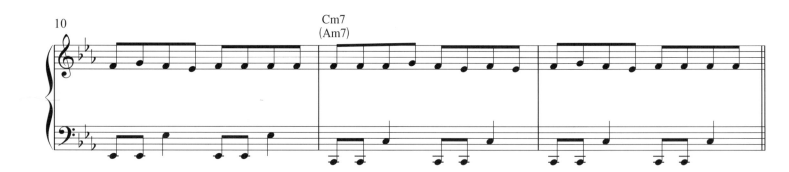

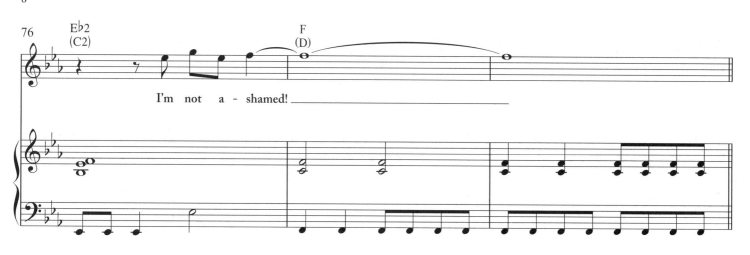

I'm not a - shamed! _____

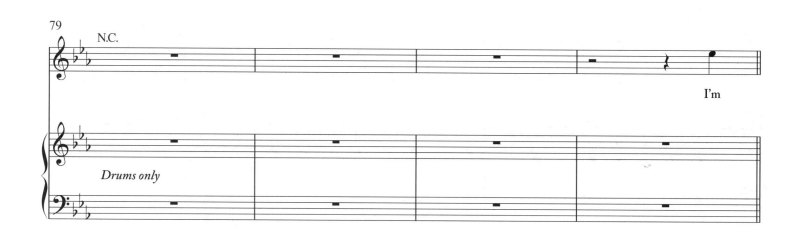

Drums only

I'm

not a - shamed of the One who saved my soul. __ I'm

not a - shamed of the One who saved my soul, my soul! __ I'm

We'll be that

OUTRO

cit-y on a hill, burn-ing bright-ly. We'll be a

light to the world, shin-ing Your glo-ry. We'll be that

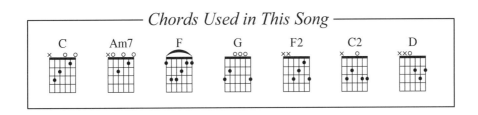

Chords Used in This Song

White Flag

Words and Music by CHRIS TOMLIN,
MATT REDMAN, MATT MAHER
and JASON INGRAM

1. The bat - tle rag - es on
2. Here on this ho - ly ground,

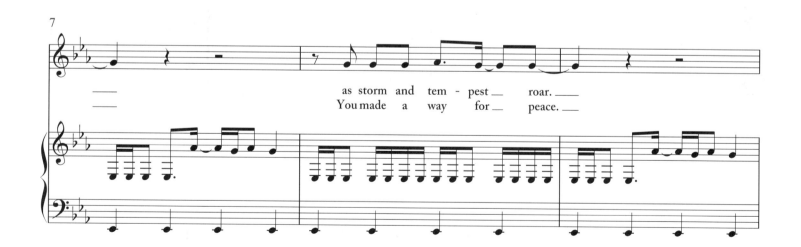

as storm and tem - pest roar.
You made a way for peace.

lift the cross, lift ___ it high, lift ___ it high! We

lift the cross, lift ___ it high, lift ___ it high! _____

OUTRO

Repeat as desired

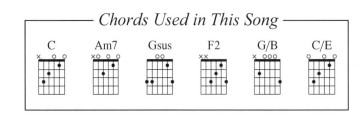

Chords Used in This Song

C Am7 Gsus F2 G/B C/E

Jesus, Son of God/How I Love You

Words and Music by CHRIS TOMLIN,
MATT MAHER and JASON INGRAM

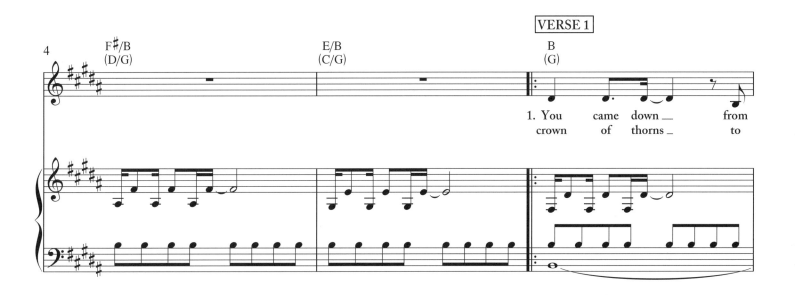

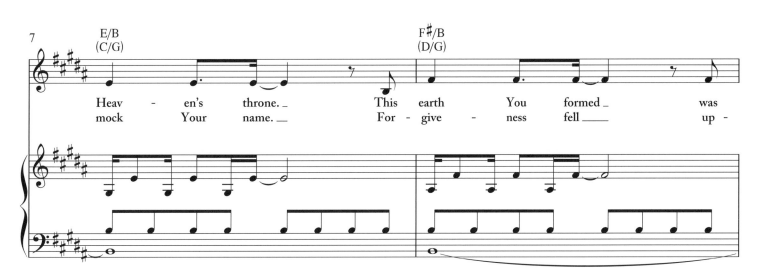

HOW I LOVE YOU
Words and Music by CHRIS TOMLIN
and CHRISTY NOCKELS

OUTRO

How I love You, love _____ You, Je - sus. How I - sus.

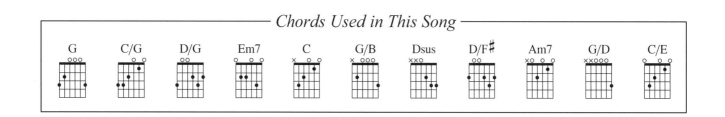

Chords Used in This Song

G   C/G   D/G   Em7   C   G/B   Dsus   D/F#   Am7   G/D   C/E

All This Glory

Words and Music by DAVID CROWDER
and LOUIE GIGLIO

Mysteriously ♩ = 95

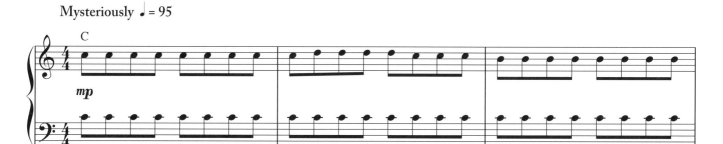

Sing 2nd time only

§ VERSE

1. In the mid-dle of the mess,
(2. In the) mid-dle of the night,

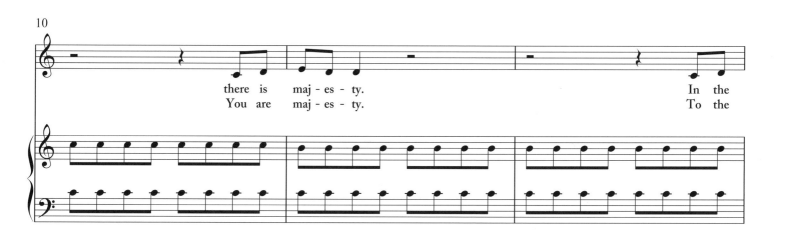

there is maj-es-ty.
You are maj-es-ty.

In the
To the

mid - dle   of   my chest   is   the   King   of   kings.
mid - dle   of   our plight   came the   King   of   kings.

While the   world was wait - ing   on   a
While   we   were wait - ing   on   Your

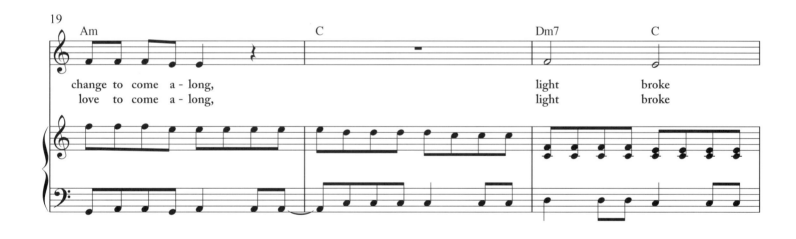

change to come a - long,   light   broke
love   to come a - long,   light   broke

2nd time to Coda

in,   com - ing like a   song.
in,   com - ing like a   Son.

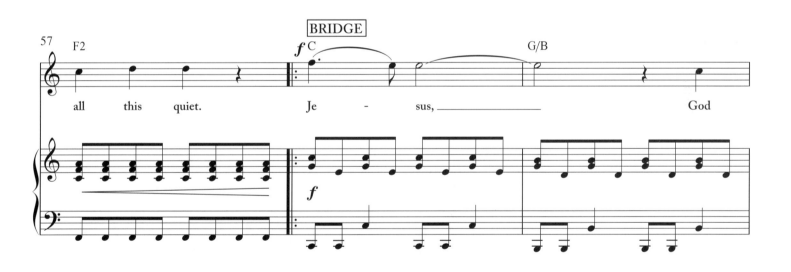

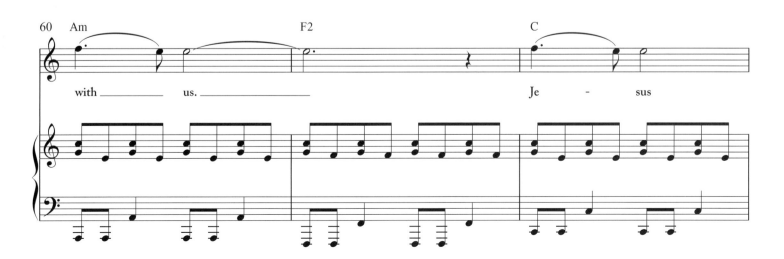

Je - sus Christ has come, and I'm un - done. love has won.

Chords Used in This Song

C   G/B   Am   Dm7   F2   C/E

Lay Me Down

Words and Music by CHRIS TOMLIN,
MATT REDMAN, JONAS MYRIN
and JASON INGRAM

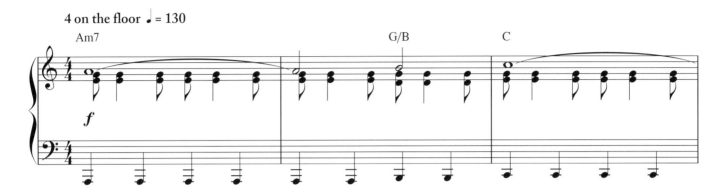

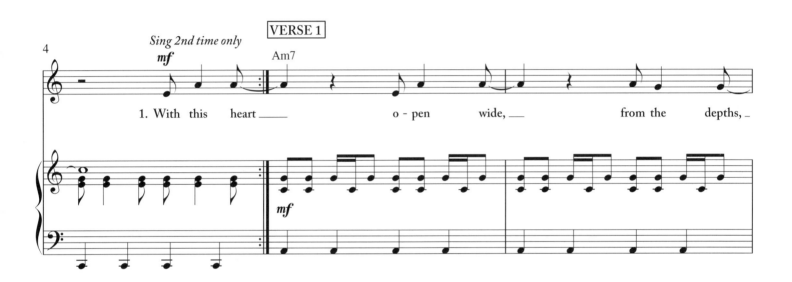

1. With this heart ___ o-pen wide, ___ from the depths, ___

___ from the heights, ___ I will bring ___ a sac-

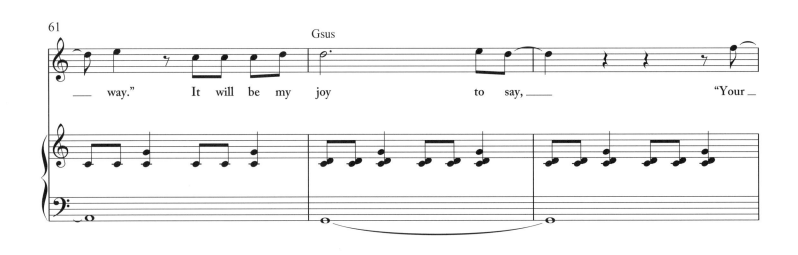

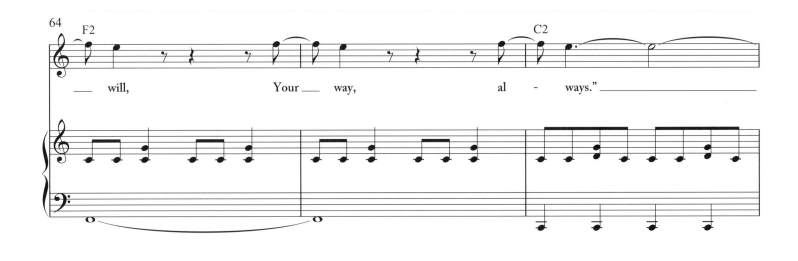

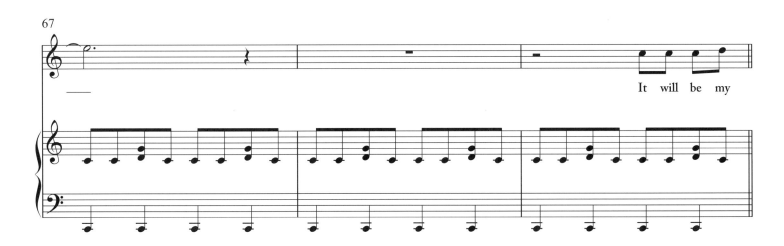

D.S. al Coda

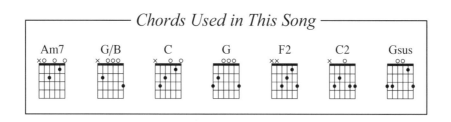

Chords Used in This Song

You Revive Me

Words and Music by CHRIS TOMLIN,
MATT MAHER and AUDREY ASSAD

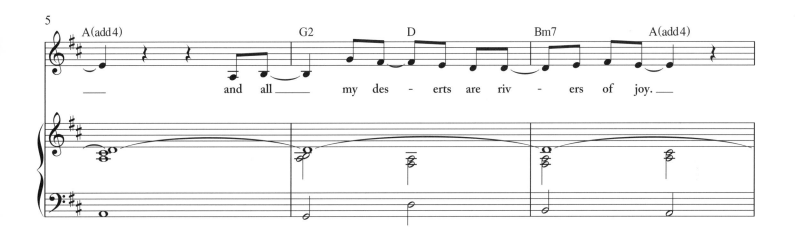

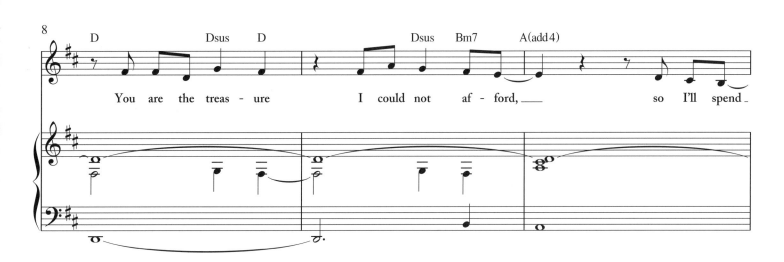

my - self ____ 'til I'm emp - ty and poor, all for You. ___

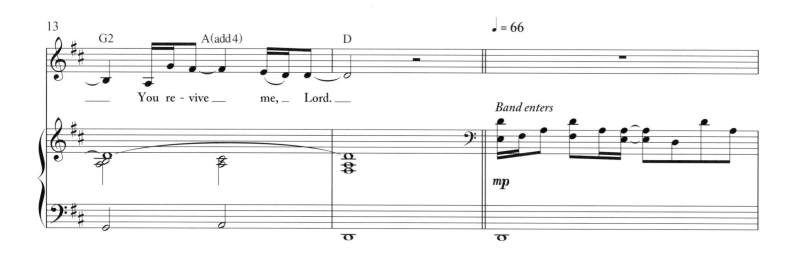

___ You re - vive ___ me, ___ Lord. ___

Band enters

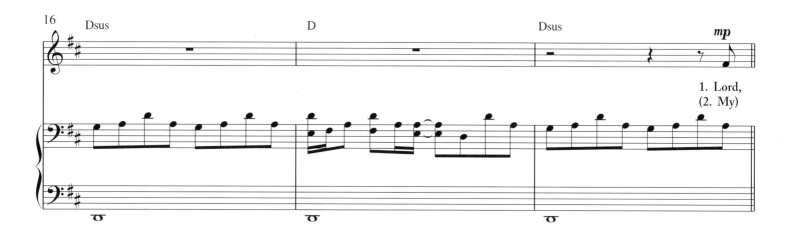

1. Lord,
(2. My)

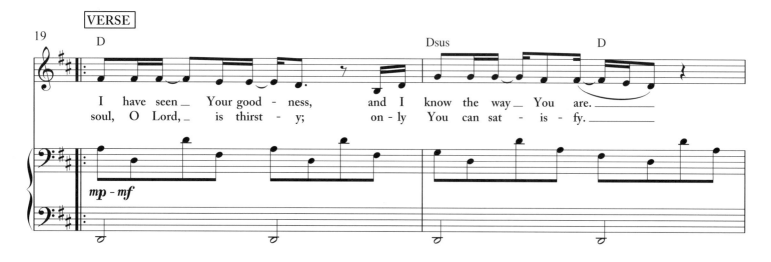

VERSE

I have seen ___ Your good - ness, and I know the way ___ You are. _____
soul, O Lord, ___ is thirst - y; on - ly You can sat - is - fy. _____

Give me eyes ___ to see ___ You in the dark. ___ And Your
You're the well ___ that nev - er will run dry. ___ And I'll

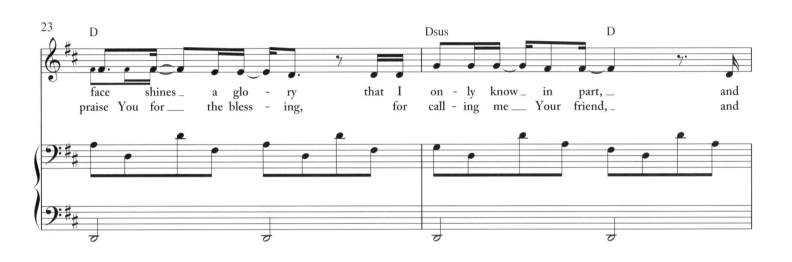

face shines ___ a glo - ry that I on - ly know ___ in part, ___ and
praise You for ___ the bless - ing, for call - ing me ___ Your friend, ___ and

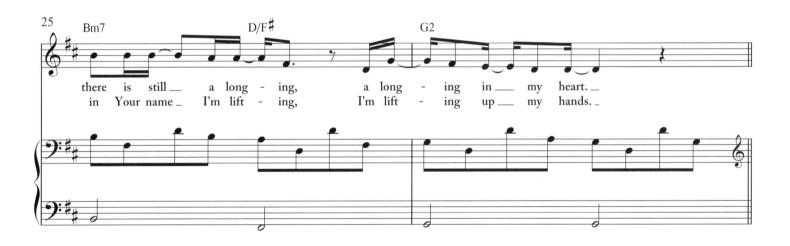

there is still ___ a long - ing, a long - ing in ___ my heart. ___
in Your name ___ I'm lift - ing, I'm lift - ing up ___ my hands. ___

CHORUS

You re - vive me, You re - vive me, ___ Lord, ___ and all ___

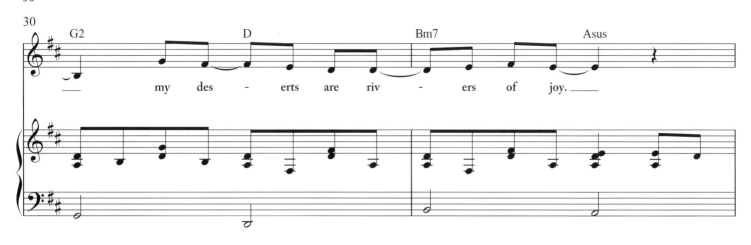

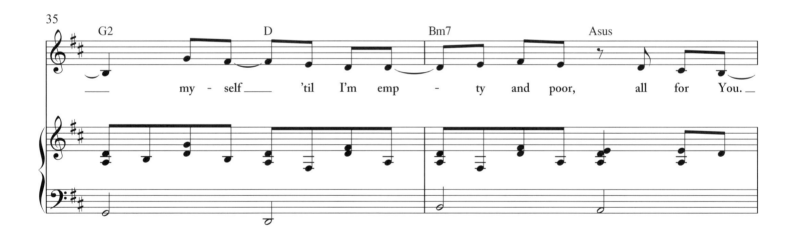

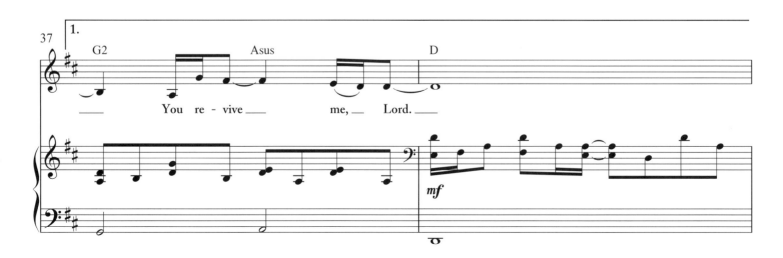

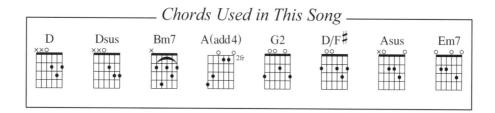

Chords Used in This Song

One Thing Remains
(Your Love Never Fails)

Words and Music by JEREMY RIDDLE,
BRIAN JOHNSON and CHRISTA BLACK

Capo 4 (G)

Mysteriously ♩ = 74

Your love —

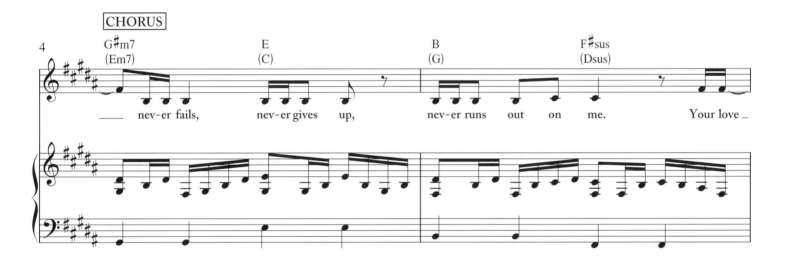

CHORUS

G#m7 (Em7) E (C) B (G) F#sus (Dsus)

— nev-er fails, nev-er gives up, nev-er runs out on me. Your love —

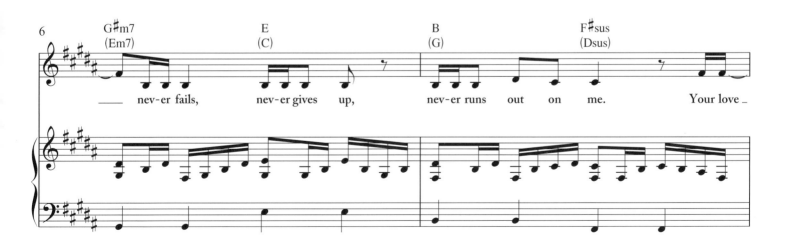

G#m7 (Em7) E (C) B (G) F#sus (Dsus)

— nev-er fails, nev-er gives up, nev-er runs out on me. Your love —

CHORUS

nev-er runs out on me, Your love. *Vocal ad lib.*

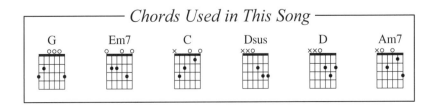

Chords Used in This Song

Yahweh

Words and Music by CHRIS TOMLIN,
JONAS MYRIN and JASON INGRAM

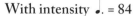

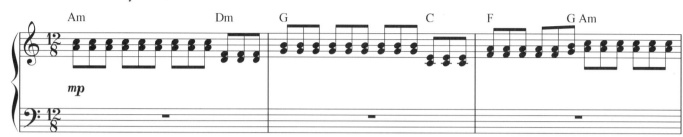

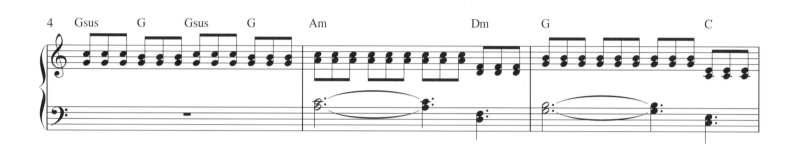

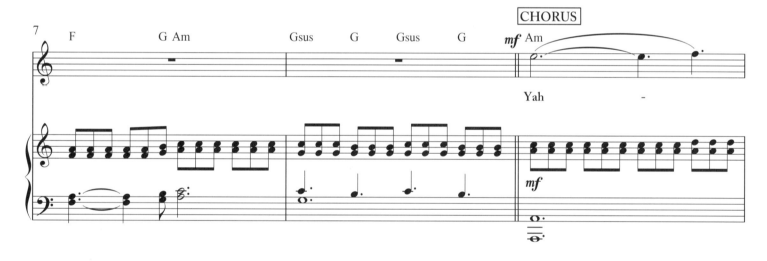

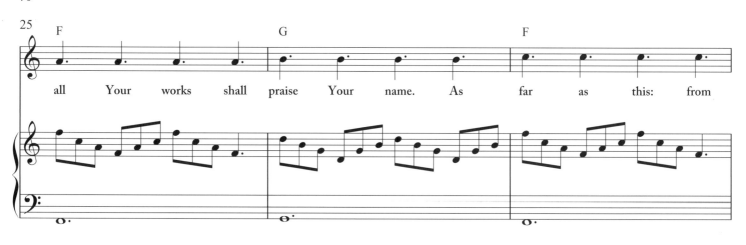

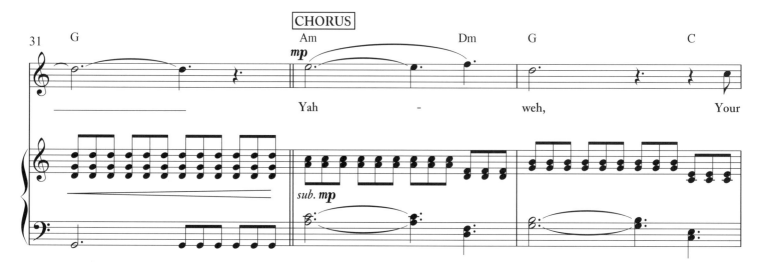

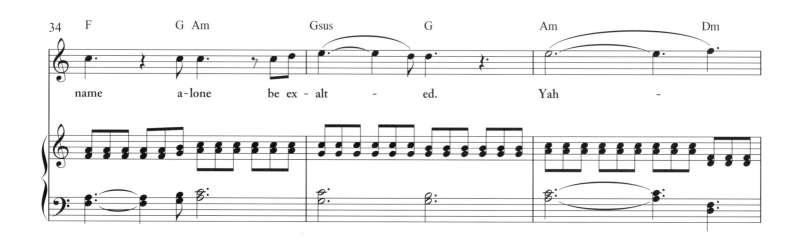

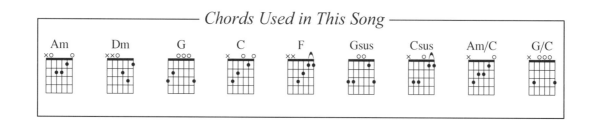

Chords Used in This Song

Am   Dm   G   C   F   Gsus   Csus   Am/C   G/C

Sing Along

Words and Music by CHRISTY NOCKELS,
NATHAN NOCKELS, JESSE REEVES,
CHRISTA BLACK and JASON INGRAM

Chords Used in This Song

The Only One

Words and Music by CHRIS TOMLIN,
DANIEL CARSON, JESSE REEVES,
MATT MAHER, MATT GILDER,
GABE SCOTT and JASON INGRAM

Capo 1 (C)

Driving ♩. = 104

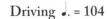

VERSE 1

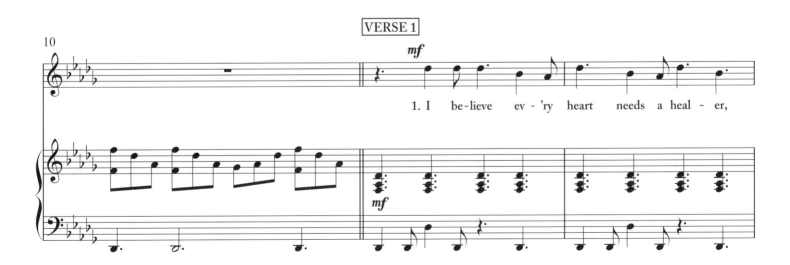

1. I be-lieve ev-'ry heart needs a heal-er,

some - one   to walk   through the fi - re. _____

INTERLUDE

I have found!

D.S. al Coda 𝄋

Chords Used in This Song

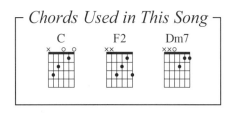

Mystery

Words and Music by
CHARLIE HALL

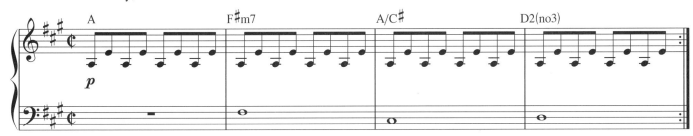

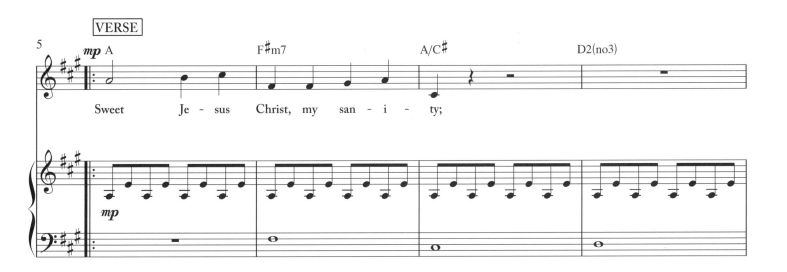

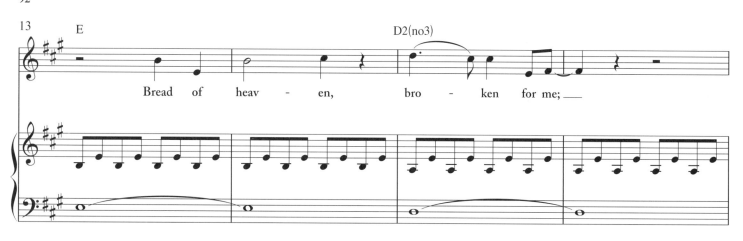

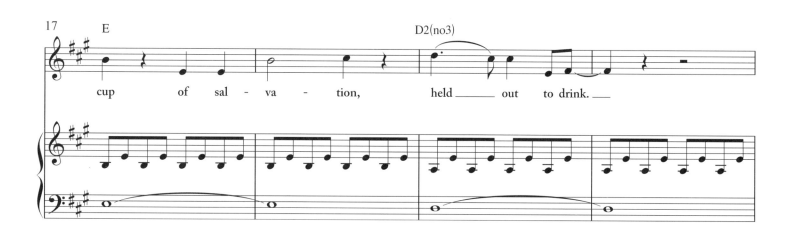

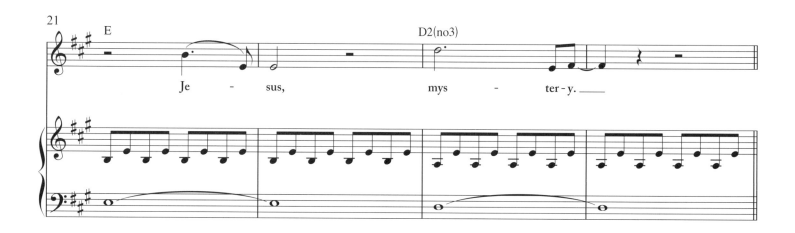

Chords Used in This Song

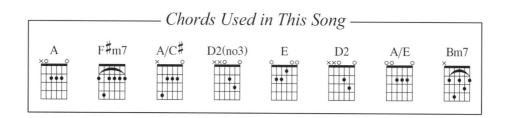

10,000 Reasons
(Bless the Lord)

Words and Music by JONAS MYRIN
and MATT REDMAN

No Turning Back

Words and Music by CHRIS TOMLIN,
MATT MAHER and JASON INGRAM

Capo 3 (C)

Moderately ♩ = 82

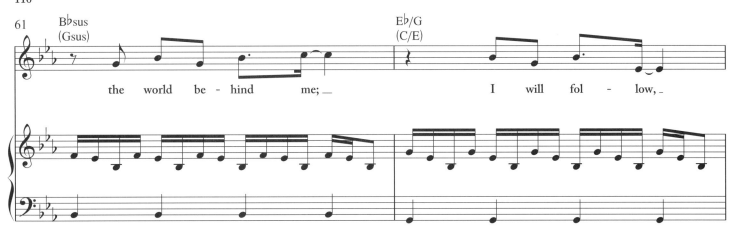

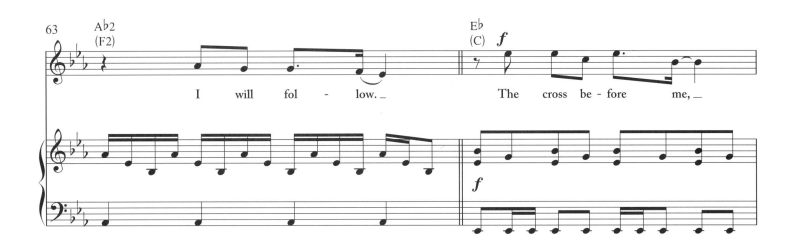

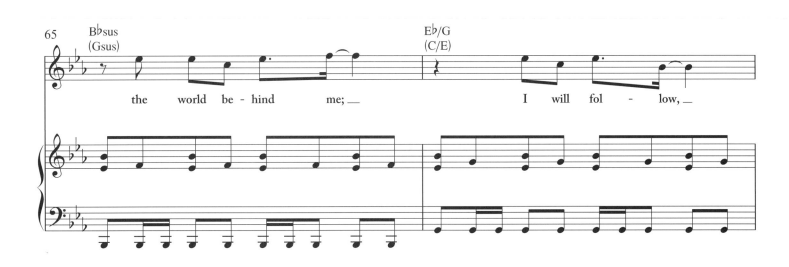

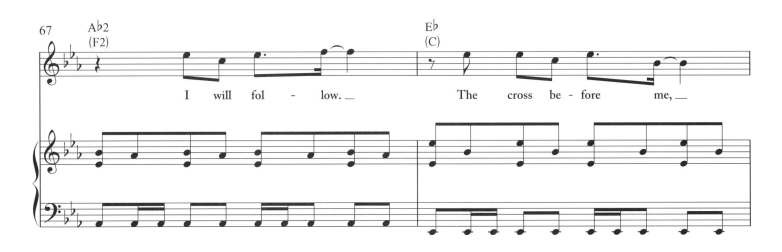

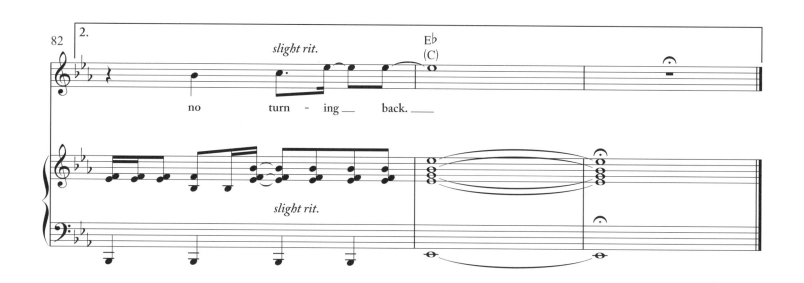

Chords Used in This Song

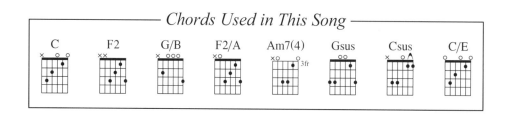